TEA WITH Grumpyboots

written by Jenny Alexander
illustrated by Tom Clayton

Chapter One

A Surprise for Sam!

Mr Green was ill for a long time. Sam kept her promise, and took his dog, Scrap, for a walk every day after school.

Mrs Green was very grateful. She always invited Sam in for a cup of tea and a slice of homemade cake, to say thank you.

Sam got to know Mrs Green very well. She wasn't at all like her husband. He always seemed so grumpy, but she was cheerful and kind. He liked to tell people off, and he never listened to what anyone said. But she was a good listener, and Sam found she could talk to her about everything.

Mr Green never had tea with them. He stayed in bed. Sometimes, Sam could hear him coughing in the room above. She was sorry he was ill, but she was glad he couldn't come down for tea, because she was frightened of him. Besides, she liked having Mrs Green to herself.

One day, when Sam took Scrap home after his walk, Mrs Green came to the door looking very happy and excited. "I've got a lovely surprise for you!" she exclaimed. "Mr Green is feeling much better today and he's decided to join us for tea!"

"Oh," said Sam, taken aback. "I mean ... Oh, good!"

Mr Green was sitting in an armchair, looking out of the window. He was wearing a dressing gown and slippers. He didn't turn round when they came in.

Mrs Green told Sam to take a seat, while she went to put the kettle on.

Sam thought she should try to be polite, so she said to Mr Green, "I'm glad you're feeling better." But he just went on gazing at the garden, ignoring her.

After that, they sat in silence. Sam wasn't going to try to talk to him if he was going to be so rude!

Chapter Two

The Secret of Mr Green's Grumpiness

At last, Mrs Green stopped rattling about in the kitchen and came through with the tea. She tapped her husband on the shoulder, and he glanced round at her.

"Would you like some tea, dear? Our young guest has arrived!"

She yelled so loudly, Sam nearly jumped out of her skin.

"He's very deaf," Mrs Green explained. "You have to get his attention first, and then talk at the top of your voice."

Mr Green appeared to notice Sam for the first time. He said a gruff hello, and thanked her for walking Scrap.

"That's all right," said Sam. "I enjoy it."

Mr Green cupped his hand behind his ear.

"I enjoy it!" Sam bellowed.

Sam explained loudly that she had always wanted a dog of her own to look after, but she couldn't have one. Looking after someone else's dog for a while was a real treat.

Mr Green nodded. "When I was your age," he said, "I wasn't allowed to have a dog, either. Then I got the chance to look after Tilly. I've got a picture of her somewhere."

He got up to look among the framed photos on the piano top. All these years she had known Mr Green, she had not realised he was deaf. It must be horrible not being able to hear what anyone was saying. No wonder he got so grumpy! No wonder he never seemed to listen!

He handed her a photo of a boy holding a little terrier like Scrap. The boy looked far too smiley to be Mr Green.

"Was her owner ill?" asked Sam. Mr Green looked at her, blankly. "Was her owner ill?" she asked again, loudly.

He shook his head. "No. I met Tilly in the war. We were both evacuated to the countryside. Tilly was an evacuee, like me."

Chapter Three

A Great Adventure

Sam knew that in the Second World War, some city children had been sent to live in the countryside, away from the bombing. But she didn't know dogs could be evacuated, too.

"Didn't the animals mind leaving their homes?"

Mr Green shrugged. “Some of them probably did,” he said. “But I think most of them were just excited by all the new sights, sounds and smells, like me. When I got on that train, I had never been on a train before in my life. It’s hard to imagine nowadays, but I had never been away from home. It was a great adventure.

Some of the other children were crying, and we had no idea where we were going. But I couldn't wait to see what the countryside was like. I had these new boots on. All the evacuees were supposed to have them, because there was so much mud in the country. I thought there would be puddles of mud everywhere, and all the people would be covered in it!

When we finally got off the train, I was really disappointed. The station was in a town, and we had to walk down an ordinary road to the reception centre, which was just a church hall. They put us all in a line, and people came to choose which children they wanted to take.

That part was not nice. I was praying I wouldn't be the last one to get chosen. But then this huge man with a red face and hairy hands stepped forward with his wife. She was nearly as big as he was and had arms as thick as tree trunks. They picked out six of the older children, including me. I was scared, I can tell you.

They had a farm outside the town. We followed them along the road, and then the houses ran out and we found ourselves in a narrow country lane. The sky was enormous, and the fields seemed to go on forever. There was so much space, it made me light-headed.

Suddenly, I was in a different world, and there was no turning back."

Chapter Four

Life on the Farm

Mr Green continued the story. "The farmer was called Mr Hardy. He expected us all to do our share of the work, because some of the farm-hands had gone to fight in the war, and he couldn't manage on his own. But we didn't mind at all. It made us feel grown up, and besides, most of the jobs we did were quite enjoyable.

One of the older boys drove the tractor. The girls helped in the kitchen, and looked after the vegetable garden. My job was helping with the animals.

Imagine! Before I went to the farm, I had never even seen a sheep, a cow or a pig. I had never seen a horse out of its harness. I thought all the animals were terrifying. I was even afraid of the chickens!

I remember the first time Mr Hardy sent me to feed them – they saw the corn bucket and came running towards me. I turned tail and ran! I thought they were attacking me."

Mr Green chuckled, remembering.

Sam said, “Was the farmer cross?”

“No. He laughed his head off. But then he made me go back.”

“Why did he choose you to look after the animals if you were so scared of them?” Sam asked. “Why didn’t he choose one of the other evacuees?”

Mr Green said that was a very interesting question, and it had a very interesting answer, too. “He chose me *because* I was scared of them. He reckoned that being afraid of them at first meant I could understand their fears. He said it would help me to treat the animals with respect. And it was true that I did seem to have a way with them.”

It was probably his gentle way with animals that drew Tilly to him. She arrived on the train a few weeks after the children. She had a label on her collar, and a letter from her owners. Months of air raids had made her nervous and unhappy, and they thought it might be better for her to be in the countryside for a while.

Chapter Five

Photos

But Tilly was very unhappy at first. She was terrified of everything. Sudden noises made her run and hide. She spent most of her time cowering in corners. The only person she would allow near her was Mr Green. He fed her and looked after her. He let her sleep on the end of his bed. He helped her to get her confidence back, and they became the firmest of friends.

Sam asked Mr Green, “Did Tilly miss her owners?”

Mr Green considered. “It’s hard to say. But they certainly missed her. They wrote to Mr Hardy and asked how she was settling in. He took this photo and sent it to them, with a note saying I was Tilly’s special friend. After that, they wrote to me.”

"Did you write back?" said Sam.

Mr Green nodded. "I told them how Tilly helped me with all my chores. I said she was frightened of the other animals at first, but that meant she never made any trouble. She didn't run at the sheep or get under the horses' hooves. She didn't chase the chickens or annoy the cows. She treated them all with respect, and they seemed to like her."

Sam wondered what happened after the war. Mr Green said Tilly stayed on the farm for several months after the children had left. Her house had been destroyed by a bomb, and her owners were homeless for a while.

He never saw her again. But he often thought about her. He wrote to Mr Hardy to see how she was getting on without him, and the farmer sent him a copy of the photo. Looking at it always reminded him of his time with Tilly on the farm.

"Happy days," he sighed. "Happy, happy days!" He smiled. Sam had never seen him smile before. She glanced at the boy in the picture, and now she could see the likeness.

Mr Green got up and put the photo back on the piano. He mumbled something, and shuffled out of the room. Scrap jumped up onto Sam's knee and Sam gave him a hug.

"Say cheese!" said Mr Green, reappearing with his camera.

A few days later, Mr Green gave Sam a copy of the photo. She was delighted. She had really enjoyed having tea with Mr Green.